You're Not for Real, Snoopy!

Selected cartoons from
You Need Help, Charlie Brown, Vol. 1

Charles M. Schulz

CORONET BOOKS
Hodder Fawcett, London

Copyright © 1964, 1965 by
United Feature Syndicate, Inc.

First published 1971 by Fawcett Publications Inc.,
New York

Coronet edition 1972
Eighth impression 1978

This book is sold subject to the condition that
it shall not, by way of trade or otherwise, be
lent, re-sold, hired out or otherwise circulated
without the publisher's prior consent in any
form of binding or cover other than that in
which this is published and without a similar
condition including this condition being
imposed on the subsequent purchaser.

Printed in Great Britain for Hodder
Fawcett Ltd., Mill Road, Dunton Green,
Sevenoaks, Kent (Editorial Office:
47 Bedford Square, London, WC1 3DP) by
C. Nicholls & Company Ltd.,
The Philips Park Press, Manchester

ISBN 0 340 15698 8

HERE...SIGN YOUR NAME ON THIS LINE..

WHEN WE GET TO SCHOOL, I'LL TAKE THIS INTO THE PRINCIPAL'S OFFICE, AND YOU WILL THEN BE OFFICIALLY ENTERED IN THE RACE FOR SCHOOL PRESIDENT!

GOOD...WE'RE ON OUR WAY!

I HOPE I WON'T BE EXPECTED TO DO SOMETHING RIGHT AWAY ABOUT TEACHERS' SALARIES...

BUT WHY DID YOU HAVE TO BRING UP THE "GREAT PUMPKIN"?

IT WAS MY DUTY, CHARLIE BROWN! HALLOWEEN WILL BE HERE IN A WEEK, AND EVERYONE SHOULD BE TOLD ABOUT THE "GREAT PUMPKIN"

OH, GOOD GRIEF!

HE RISES OUT OF THE PUMPKIN PATCH WITH HIS BAG OF TOYS, AND FLIES THROUGH THE AIR BRINGING JOY TO ALL THE CHILDREN OF THE WORLD!

YOU'RE LOOKING AT ME LIKE I'M CRAZY..

I'M LOOKING AT YOU LIKE I COULD HAVE BEEN VICE-PRESIDENT!

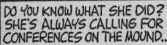

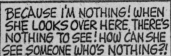

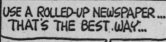

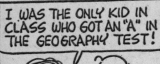

MY TEACHER, MISS OTHMAR, IS GOING TO PUT IN FOR A SALARY CHANGE

A SALARY CHANGE?

YES, SHE SAYS SHE TAKES CHILDREN TO THE MOVIE ROOM FOR MOVIES, TO THE ART ROOM FOR ART, BACK TO THE MOVIE ROOM FOR FILM STRIPS...

TO THE LIBRARY FOR BOOKS, TO THE CAFETERIA FOR LUNCH, TO THE GYM FOR PHYSICAL EDUCATION AND AROUND AND AROUND THE SCHOOL BUILDING FOR YARD DUTIES...

SHE'S DECIDED SHE WANTS TO BE PAID BY THE MILE!

SCHULZ

SNOOPY, HOW ABOUT GOING FOR A LITTLE WALK IN THE PARK?

GREAT!

I'M ALWAYS AFRAID TO GO FOR A WALK ALONE... I MIGHT GET MUGGED!

FOR THE LOVE OF PEANUTS

All these books are available at your local bookshop or newsagent, or can be ordered direct from the publisher. Just tick the titles you want and fill in the form below.
Prices and availability subject to change without notice.

CORONET BOOKS, P.O. Box 11, Falmouth, Cornwall.

Please send cheque or postal order, and allow the following for postage and packing:
U.K. – One book 22p plus 10p per copy for each additional book ordered, up to a maximum of 82p.
B.F.P.O. and EIRE – 22p for the first book plus 10p per copy for the next 6 books, thereafter 4p per book.
OTHER OVERSEAS CUSTOMERS – 30p for the first book and 10p per copy for each additional book.

Name ....

Address ....

....